Creating a Timeline for Your Book

Beyond the Basics

Connie Dunn

Creating a Timeline for Your Book: Beyond the Basics by Connie Dunn, Copyright © 2014

Published by Nature Woman Wisdom Press

First Edition. Printed and bound in the United States of America

ISBN-13: 978-0615968278
ISBN-10: 0615968279
9 8 7 6 5 4 3 2

Dunn, Connie
Creating a Timeline for Your Book: Beyond the Basics

Books
> *Creating a Timeline for Your Book: Beyond the Basics*
> *Connie Dunn*

Book Writing
> *Creating a Timeline for Your Book: Beyond the Basics*
> *Connie Dunn*

Writing
> *Creating a Timeline for Your Book: Beyond the Basics*
> *Connie Dunn*

Table of Contents

Introduction

One thing to know about books is that everything takes a different amount of time for each manuscript and person. However, knowing that this is ONLY a guideline, you can hopefully use it to estimate your own timeline.

I've been writing books since 1981. Each book that I have written since then has taken progressively less time. I account most of that to the technology changes.

My Publishing Experience

In 1981, when I published a cookbook, I typed all of the recipes into my computer, printed them out, and then mailed them in an envelope to a typesetter.

When I got my pages back (also mailed through the US Postal Service), I then had to assemble my pages. I made quite a few mistakes in doing my cookbook, but for a first-time project, I suppose I did pretty well.

Timeline Overview

1	2	3	4	5	6	7	8	9	10	11	12	13	14	15	16	17	18	19	20	21	22	23	24	25	26	27	28	29	30	31	32	33	34	35	36

Writing Can Take Somewhere Between 1 and 36 Months or More

Editing Can Take Between 1 Day to 1 Month, Depending on Your Manuscript's Length and Accuracy

Normally, an Editor Will Ask to See the First 10 Pages Before Giving You an Estimate of Cost

This Process Can ONLY Be Done Once You Are Finished Writing and Doing Some Editing of Content, Sentence Structure, Punctuation, and Spelling – this Is Your Pass Through Your Manuscript to Make It as Clean as Possible! Editors charge approx. $55/hr.

Average Manuscript Takes Between 1-10 Hours, But Can Take Much Longer

Formatting and Publishing – I Suggest Formatting as Soon as Possible, I Start from the Beginning

If You Have Not, then This Process Can Be Done in Conjunction with Your Editing or

It Is Another Pass through Your Manuscript. Decisions for Formatting: Font Type and Size of Fonts for Body Text, Table of Contents, Headings 1- 3, plus Cover Items (Title, Subtitle, Byline) and Other Unique Items in Your Manuscript. This Is Generally Done via a Tagging System, which Makes It Easy to Change the Formatting and Look of Your Book by Manipulation of Tags.

Marketing Can Start when YOU Begin the Writing Process, But May Extend Up to 36 Months or More

PRE-MARKETING Begins When You Begin Writing

The Writing Timeline

Writing is a process. Books and writers do not necessarily fit into any standard boxes, because each book you write has its own challenges along with life challenges while you are trying to write.

The Writing Timeline includes:
- Outlining
- Title Decisions
- Searching for the right PROBLEM/HOOK to begin your book.

Writing is a process. Books and writers do not necessarily fit into any standard boxes, because each book you write has its own challenges along with life challenges while you are trying to write.

The Writing Timeline includes:
- Outlining
- Title Decisions
- Searching for the right PROBLEM/HOOK to begin your book.

A book can take from 1 to 36 months to write, depending on the topic, genre, and your ability to discipline your writing schedule.

There are many variables. Everyone writes at a different rate.

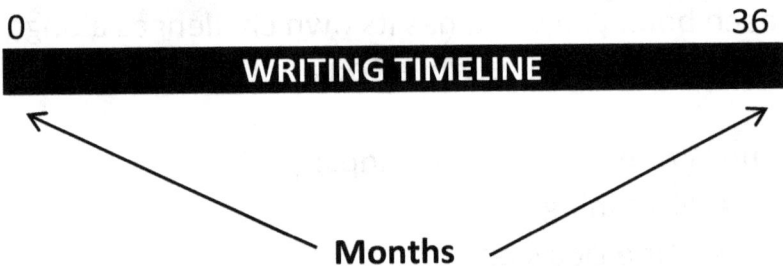

0   36

WRITING TIMELINE

Months

Understanding what goes into the Writing Process will help you set achievable GOALS that hopefully will fall into this Timeline. However, if it doesn't, don't worry, just keep working and setting GOALS and meeting the goals.

Having an accountability partner can help you stay on-track.

Editing Timeline

Editing can put you into a Black Hole from which you have a hard time returning. During the editing process is when most people get stuck in the perfection mode.

When you strive for perfection, it's hard to stop. When is your manuscript really "perfect?" Errors are a fact of life in the publishing world. You somehow have to accept "good enough" at some point or you'll be 10 or more years down the road and still working on the same book!

Understanding what goes into the Editing Process will help you set appropriate goals for your own part of the editing.

The process for getting your book manuscript professionally edited takes somewhere between 1 and 4 weeks. This depends on how long the manuscript is, and accuracy level. If punctuation and spelling aren't your thing, then the editor will fix it. The more work, the longer it will take and the higher the cost.

1   4

EDITING TIMELINE

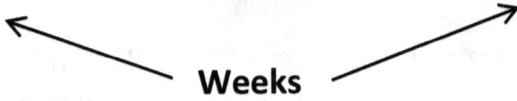

Weeks

Formatting Timeline

The Formatting Timeline is usually the shorter of all the processes. I usually format as I go, so by the end of my writing process, I am pretty much done with formatting.

I always go back through the manuscript to make sure that everything really looks consistent.

Formatting is an important step in making your manuscript ready for publishing. This is the process in which I add most of the art that is going into the book.

I also make sure page breaks are in the right place.

1   5
FORMATTING TIMELINE
Weeks

Publishing Timeline

Unless you have problems within your file, this process is often just as quick or quicker than the formatting process. If all goes right, this can be done within an hour. See the Publishing Process to get more details about publishing using such on-demand online publishing/printers as CreateSpace.com.

1   3

PUBLISHING TIMELINE

Hours

Marketing Timeline

The Marketing Timeline is as long or longer than the writing process. While it is a good idea to begin marketing while you are still writing, I have to acknowledge how difficult this can be. See the Marketing Process for more details into what this involves.

1   36

MARKETING TIMELINE

Weeks

Today's Technology: The Writer's Role

More technology allows us to do things in a much quicker manner. It also means that the writer has taken on all the roles up to the actual printing.

Today, we have electronic printing devices that are so sophisticated that it can print and bind an entire book from a simple electronic file. Perhaps, that's an over-simplification of the electronic printing process. There is little done by humans in this process, which makes it much cheaper.

Processes Overview

Let's take a look at all the processes involved in making a book in today's electronic age:
1. Writing
2. Editing
3. Formatting for Publishing
4. Publishing Process with the On-Demand publishing/printing company
5. Marketing

While the PROCESSES have really not changed in that they all still take place, these are now all heaped upon the writer. So if you feel a bit overwhelmed by all the work it takes to publish your book, remember that each separate process used to be done by someone other than you, the writer!

Okay, don't get too carried away! You see, it also means we are in control of all of this, as well.

Before, we would send off our manuscript and not see any progress or sign that our book was moving forward for perhaps one or two years! We would get what they called galley proofs, which was the first thing that we would see of our yet unpublished book.

At that point, major changes would be too costly, so the publisher would not approve those. Minor changes, such as typos were fixed.

Now, in our wonderful electronic world, we can go from writing to publishing in a very short time.

The secret to cutting down the time is starting your book in the format that you will use.

Writing Process

Writing Process – the process of putting one word after another to form sentences and paragraphs. As you are writing a book, your use of words to communicate laughter, tears, and other emotions can all be done through the combination of words.

Writing can either be a delightful experience or painful. That can be related to your content or just your struggle with writing.

If you would rather speak than write, then try your hand at speaking into a digital recording device or use Dragon Speaks and other MP3 recording software. Once you have an MP3 file, you can send that to a transcriptionist, who will transcribe your words into a printable form. You may need to clean it up a bit, because we don't speak with the same flow as we write. Our thoughts are often more scattered when talking, yet probably more authentic.

We all communicate with our clients and customers, students and fellow teachers, friends and family. The material you are writing may be associated with your business or work. Therefore, you are the right person to write this book! Writing and speaking are modes of communicating.

Humanity communicates in a myriad of manners, some we cannot easily communicate in either speech or writing. That is where the craft of writing comes into our writing process.

Foreshadowing – the art of giving hints of what is to come without giving away the suspense.

Foreshadowing - To present an indication or suggestion beforehand or to foretell an event before it happens.

For example: *On a dark, and stormy night, the girl shivered under her covers.* This is somewhat of a cliché opening for many novels. I hope you avoid this particular string of words.

However, the foreshadowing comes from the suggestion that something is going to happen. What? We don't know.

But when it does happen, we're ready for it. Why? The setting of a dark and stormy night usually means lights go out and it's spooky! Now give us the girl shivering under the covers. We know why she shivers, something is about to happen.

Using foreshadowing can make your writing interesting and intriguing. You can be clever about dropping these hints of what is to come.

It can be a thought one of your characters has, depending on your point of view. It can be the way you describe the environment or the way a character behaves.

But when it does happen, we're ready for it. Why? The setting of a dark and stormy night usually means lights go out and it's spooky! Now give us the girl shivering under the covers. We know why she shivers, something is about to happen.

Using foreshadowing can make your writing interesting and intriguing. You can be clever about dropping these hints of what is to come.

It can be a thought one of your characters has, depending on your point of view. It can be the way you describe the environment or the way a character behaves.

The *breadcrumb* method allows you to drop tiny pieces all through your manuscript that leads your readers to the final resolution.

Like in the use of actual breadcrumbs to leave a trail that you can retrace, such as the one used in the folktale *Hansel and Gretel*. Foreshadowing can work early in your story, but later you can use breadcrumbs to drop clues that take you to the end.

Breadcrumbs - Tiny pieces of bread is the official definition. However, this technique used in writing or telling stories. It is like dropping actual pieces of bread along a trail that you can follow. Instead of actual "bread," these breadcrumbs are little clues that help readers follow the thread of the story to the end.

Another way to explain this is: having an ending that returns to the beginning. Using the breadcrumbs, like the foreshadowing, keeps the reader engaged in the story.

For example: (Beg.) Making puppets requires knowledge of characters. What makes them interesting are not the major construction but in the small details, such as a unique smile, shape and size of eyes, and possibly a facial anomaly like a mole or birth mark. (End) The puppet creator catches the nuances of a person's character, which allows her to make puppets that are replicas of individuals.

Cliff Hangers – the art of leaving a story hanging on a cliff or by the toenails even! We are at the end of the story, but you've left your readers wanting to know more. But what happens after...

This is a great technique to use at the end of chapters, because readers want to read to the end of a chapter before they put the book down. What happens when you leave a cliff hanger is that the reader has to read the next chapter.

I've been known to read a book from cover to cover in one sitting without stopping, because the cliff hangers kept pulling me through the story. When you're done, you usually say: "Wow! That was a GREAT story!"

While there are many great writing techniques, this lesson cannot present them all. This Wikipedia site does a pretty good job of listing and explaining them: http://en.wikipedia.org/wiki/Literary_technique

Editing – the process of correcting errors, which is actually more the definition of "Copyediting." However, the process of editing includes "Copyediting," as well as making your manuscript more readable by clearing up awkward wording.

"Content" editing is part of the editing process, which is more of a content management issue. The flow of the manuscript is included in the "Content" editing.

When I think of editing, I see it as two-fold. The first part is my responsibility to go through it and make it as perfect as I can make it. The second part is getting it edited by a professional editor.

Will it be perfect once you've had it edited? No, probably not! It's not that your editor is bad or that you are. The fact is that errors just creep in and get overlooked.

Sometimes you simply have to say "good enough, is good enough!" Otherwise, you could be working on your book for 10 or more years. At some point, you simply have to let it go and allow it to be published.

Perfection can be an obstacle to publishing, but I'm not suggesting that you ignore errors when you see them. Just don't make yourself crazy over perfection; you owe it to yourself!

Formatting Process

Format – the process of creating continuity of fonts and font size.

If you are familiar with the templates on your word processing software, you can easily create a unique template for your book.

Decide what font type and size that you want your "Normal Text" or "Body Text" to be. For example, *Comic Sans* is a Font Type. The size is measured in points, such as 8-72 point.

"Normal Text" or "Body Text" for book use is usually between 10 and 12. For children's books, the main body text might be more like 14 or 16, in some cases up to 18.

You need to choose what font and size your Headings 1, 2, and 3 will be. Headings can be a different font, but is usually compatible. For example, if you font is *Arial*, you might choose *Arial Black* for headings. *Arial* is a *sans serif* font, so you could match another sans serif font with *Arial* for headings.

Book Title, Subtitle, Byline, Table of Contents, and Copyright Page are other choices that you need to decide fonts and size.

Now that you've made these decisions, you are almost ready to go through your manuscript and apply them.

But not yet...you still need to choose a "trim size."

Trim Size – the size of your finished book. It is referred to as the "trim" size, because it is printed on slightly larger paper and is trimmed to the appropriate size.

Common "Trim" Sizes are 6-inches by 9-inches, 5-inches by 8-inches, 5.25-inches by 8-inches, and 5.5-inches by 8.5-inches. This is not all the "Trim" Sizes available, just the most commonly used.

Now, you are ready to begin your formatting. To select your *Page Size*, go to *Page Layout*, select *Page Size*. You may need to select a *Custom Page Size*. To do this, scroll down for more size choices. You may need to do this twice before you get to the screen where you can enter your "custom" size.

Publishing Process

Depending on your "Publishing Choice," this could be the easiest process of all.
While the choices include:

- **Traditional Publishing** (if you have chosen this, you don't need to go past the first editing that you do, skip this process altogether, but skip to marketing...this is necessary no matter what route you go!)

- **Self-publishing** is basically like "Traditional Publishing" only you pay exorbitant fees...Don't go this route! These Publishers are "Vanity" Presses.

Independent or **Indie Publishing** is when you choose to publish on your own terms. There are choices under this banner, which include:

- CreateSpace, Lulu, Xilibris, and other on-demand publishers/printers.

Please note that the prices on these publishers/printers are not the same prices. In my investigation, CreateSpace has the lowest fees, as of Feb.2014.

- LightningSource, which is an on-demand printer, which means you have to be your own indie publishing company. They offer many more choices in paper - higher grades of paper - trim sizes, etc. This will be more money than the CreateSpace publisher/printer. There is either a setup fee or a minimum number of books to order.

Local or Regional printers, which offer full print and binding options. Large array of papers and textures, including after print coatings. These will cost a premium. There will be larger out of pocket costs up-front.

Once you choose your mode of publishing, they each have their progression of tasks. Each of these options offers you to submit your file via e-mail or upload, which cuts the time delay for snail mail or in-person delivery.

Costs and time elements differ from each provider.

I will walk you through the process from CreateSpace, which will illustrate similar processes from other on-demand publishers or printers.

Process for Create Space.

1. Set up an account at CreateSpace.com or sign into your account.
2. On the CreateSpace Dashboard, choose New Book.
3. You will be asked to enter the Title and Subtitle.
4. Under Contributors, enter the author's name or authors' names. Add your Illustrator's Name, and choose "Illustrator."
5. You will be asked for the number of pages for your book.
6. You will be asked to:
   - Enter an ISBN (International Standard Book Number), which you can get at MyIdentifiers.com (price is $125 for one, $250 for 10);
   - Allow CreateSpace to assign one as your PUBLISHER; or

- Purchase your ISBN through CreateSpace as your own Publishing Company at a low rate of $10. This is a one-time fee.

7. Add your ISBN on the Copyright Page.
8. Take your file, which has been edited and formatted for the trim size you have chosen, and turn it into a .pdf file. If you can print to .pdf, that usually offers you a higher resolution file. Go into printer options on your print menu and choose "High, for Print." This is the highest resolution and it also embeds your fonts.
9. Choose your Trim Size, which should match the formatting that you've done in your .pdf file.
10. Upload your .pdf file as the INTERIOR of your book.
11. Review it through the online reviewer. If you are satisfied with the file, click on SKIP Review. If you need to make corrections, do that and resave or reprint it to .pdf with the HIGH PRINT MODE and upload it again. Repeat the review process. Repeat this entire process until you are satisfied with your file.

12. Review the book with the cover. You can repeat this process as many times as you need to get it to the point you are satisfied.
13. Choose, SKIP REVIEW to move to the next choice.
14. Create your Book Cover
15. Use the Online Cover Creator, using one of the templates.
16. Create your own original Cover, using the dimensions given or one of the blank templates.
17. Choosing your DISTRIBUTION is the last choice. Sign up for everything you can!
18. There is a $35 charge on CreateSpace for Expanded Distribution. This is a one-time fee.
19. Set your PRICE for your book.
20. CreateSpace will review your file, once approved, you can begin ordering books.

Marketing Process

The Marketing Process needs to start even before you have published your book, if possible.

Try to sell pre-publication copies.

Set up a Website for your book. Begin collecting e-mail addresses and a blog that would appeal to your target readers.

Create partnerships with organizations that make sense for your book. Note: Not all books lend themselves to this!

Look at other Blogs that appeal to your same target audience. Comment and develop a relationship with the Blogger.

Fiction writers can do this! You simply blog about your characters or even have your characters write the blog.

The point of this is to develop a following.

When your book is published, it will go out on Amazon.com. Go to https://authorcentral.amazon.com/ to set up your author page.

The Virtual Blog Tour is one of the best ways to market your book, according to most of the book marketing experts.

The simple explanation of this is to find blogs that target your same audience. Ask to be a "guest blogger." Try to find blogs across the country. There is much more to be said about this. However, this information will be presented to you in a separate course.

The Writing Plan

A Writing Plan is where you break down the processes, create your own personalized TIMELINE and GOAL SETTING.

It is similar to a Business or Marketing Plan, but since your goal is more focused on one book product, it may look more like a Project Management Report than either a Business or Marketing Plan.

The elements that you need to address in your writing plan are:

1. Topic of Book
2. Outline of Book
3. Title or Title Selections (pick one as a working title)
4. Goals for Writing
5. Timeline for Writing
6. Goals for Editing and Formatting
7. Timeline for Editing and Formatting
8. Goals for Publishing
    1. Choose Method (Traditional or Independent)
    2. Your Target Audience (Who You Are Writing for)
9. Timeline for Publishing

10. Goals for Marketing
    1. Where does your Target Audience Hang Out?
    2. How will you reach your Target Audience?
    3. Explore Marketing Options
        1. Virtual Book Tour
        2. Book Signings
        3. Advertising
        4. Other
11. Timeline for Marketing

About the Author

Connie Dunn is an author, speaker, educator and owner of Publish with Connie and Nature Woman Wisdom Press. She writes courses, such as her signature, "12 Easy Steps to Publishing."

Connie also writes children's books, such as her collection of children's stories, "A Spider, Some Thread, and a Labyrinth Walk," and non-fiction, such as "12 Steps to Publishing: Workbook," "Press Releases Made Easy."

She has more than 25 years of experience in writing for magazines and newspapers. She had a regular column in the Dallas Morning News, which focused on small and home-based businesses. For this column, she won an award from the SBA (Small Business Administration). Connie also developed courseware for a number of start-up technology firms. She worked with publishers, such as Prentice Hall and Taylor Publishing as a Developmental (content) Editor. She self-published her first book in 1981, and developed a collection of stories with a collaborator in the 1990s. She writes children's books, non-fiction, and fiction. Connie believes that everyone has a book in them and her greatest joy is in traveling with her students on their writing journeys.

Books Available from Connie Dunn

Each book has a page on www.naturewomanwisdom.com under the books tab and a link from that page.

A Spider, Some Thread, and a Labyrinth Walk
Book Writing: Fuzzy About Where to Start?
Destiny Has Two Grandmas: Why Do Things Change?
Goddess Rituals: Reclaiming Our Ancient Spiritual Heritage
Lights for Luucy
Miss Odell: The Privileges of Being Present for the End of Her Life - A Reality Book on Elder Care
Press Releases Made Easy
The Fairies of Ferry Beach
The Most Magical, Awesome, Delicate Creature of All
The Real Story of the Dumpty Family
Trees: Peaceful and Personal Meditational Poems
When Rusty Went Driving
Zoe

The End

www.ingramcontent.com/pod-product-compliance
Lightning Source LLC
Chambersburg PA
CBHW071234290326
41931CB00037B/2939